Clare Hannah Ellin
1904 - 1984

ISBN 978-1-904446-72-9

For Ruth

Published and printed by
Quacks Books
7 Grape Lane
Petergate
York YO1 7HU

Contents

Introduction

In September of 1978 Clare Ellin published a little book of thirty-eight of her poems under the title "*East Riding Heritage*". The opening page explained:

"This is our East Riding
treasure it with pride
its dialect, humour, history –
held by coast and rivers
and fringed by Humberside."

"Many of the poems in this collection
have been previously published in the
Yorkshire Post or broadcast on B.B.C. radio
or television."

Thirty-four years later, in 2012, when my wife Elsie and I came to live in Kilnwick I was given a copy of a poem about the ha-ha that was originally part of the Kilnwick Hall estate and which now forms a part of our front garden. Having been a city-dweller for most of my life I didn't know what a ha-ha was and had to reach immediately for my copy of *Collins English Dictionary.*

The Ha-ha, Kilnwick

There's a man, see, planting a tree
where no tree should be,
for the Lord of the Manor did once decree
that no tree should impede his view.

He built a ha-ha of rosy bricks
with a ditch to fence his cattle,
then he watched from tall windows
the vagrants pass, tinkers and gypsies,
his men returning from their labours
and the to-ing and fro-ing
of friends and neighbours.
He could see the coach at Horn Hill Top
in time to don his beaver hat
and his Sunday-best cravat.
He's been gone this long time past,
so has his hall with windows tall
but the rosy-bricked ha-ha will last
as long as the dog rose veils its decay
and the man and the tree
have gone their way.

I had no idea who had written this verse. It was only much later that I learned that the poem came from Clare Ellin's little grey book *"East Riding Heritage".* Although the book was long out of print I managed to buy a copy of it online.

Being a curious sort of cove I wanted to know more about this lady poet, this East Yorkshire lass, called Clare Ellin. Where did she live? What else had she written? Was she still alive? I began my enquiries with my neighbour Richard Benwell of Kilnwick Gardens, who has lived in the village all his life. *"Oh, yes"* Richard told me, *"I know who Clare Ellin was. She lived here in Kilnwick – at Oaks Cottage on Main Street - and was a friend of my mother's".*

Richard went on to tell me how he had kept in touch for many years with Clare Ellin's daughter, Ruth Brown, who lives in Derbyshire. My wife Elsie and I were then able to visit Ruth and learn so much more about her mother's life and work.

Ruth herself is also a talented artist who painted porcelain until a stroke cruelly left her left hand – her painting hand – unable to paint any more. We really enjoyed chatting to Ruth in her Belper bungalow. She is a wonderful lady of eighty-five now. Happily her son Robert lives close by.

As I began to read more of what Clare has written, I could see that she was much more than just an occasional poet. She was deeply interested in the people and places of the East Riding. She was a countrywoman, a photographer, a local historian, journalist and public speaker. She was an expert on the dialects of East Yorkshire and a member of the Yorkshire Dialect Society. She was a regular contributor to Yorkshire's newspapers and local radio and TV programmes.

Second to her writing, Clare's great passion was gardening and she wrote about that too. She had a good marriage, full of love and good humour.

There are a few Kilnwick folk still around who knew Clare personally. But many residents, just like I was, are unaware of the 'Wise Woman of Kilnwick'. She deserves to be remembered. That is why I feel it is important to write this little biographical essay about our only published poet. Her book of poems was entitled *"East Riding Heritage"* but Clare herself is an important part of that heritage.

Dialect or English?

In 1844 the Dorset preacher-poet William Barnes became very popular when he published a collection of poems in Dorset dialect. Some years later he took pity on those who could neither speak nor understand Dorset and produced another collection of verse written in what he called 'Common English'. This brought his work to a much larger audience.

Like William Barnes, our Kilnwick poet, Clare Ellin, also wrote partly in dialect and partly in plain English. And just as we can't understand the Dorset dialect poems of William Barnes, the general, non-northern reader might have difficulty comprehending some of the Clare Ellin poems re-produced in the Transactions of the Yorkshire Dialect Society, for example. In this selection of Clare's verse I have tried to avoid the linguistically more challenging poems.

One of my favourite Clare Ellin poems is *To My Sister*. Last year my wife and I decided to reprint this poem in our personal Christmas card. But as many of our friends are not northcountry folk, and some are not even British, we felt we needed to present it in plainer English for them. So authenticity was sacrificed for comprehension.

This nostalgic poem gives a good insight into Clare's early childhood. Her sister Dorothy was two years younger than Clare. Although the poem is describing a Christmas morning as it was in 1910 or thereabouts, it is very similar to my own experience of Christmas as a child, in the Hull of the 1930s, when I also believed in Father Christmas. Oh, happy days of innocence!

This is my 'anglicized' version:

To My Sister

Do you remember Christmases when we were little lasses?
We helped our mam to make mince-pies, and then we polished t'brasses.
We shined up candlesticks so bright, and put new candles in
For mam to light on Christmas night when Santa Claus came in.
And then we got a pie apiece and put our own mark on 'em,
And set 'em up on t'chimneypiece for Santa Claus to get 'em.
We hung our stockings up on t'post at bottom end o' t'bed,
And then we tried to get to sleep because our father said:
"Any bairn that Santa hinders, gets her stocking full of cinders!"

When we woke on Christmas morn we had no candlelight,
We got our stockings off the post and guessed with all our might,
And then we shouted to our mam to let us have a light.
She came, with candle in her hand, her nightgown long and white,
She sat on t'bed and watched us undoing all the strings,
She seemed as thrilled as we were with all our little things.
There were packs of chocolate pennies, and sugar-candy pigs,
And goodies, nuts, and apples, and red-tipped sugar cigs,
And down at very bottom, when we thought we'd got all t'things,
A little conny box apiece, with two real golden rings!

And then we packed them up again and tried to get to sleep,
But I kept thinking o' t'mince-pies and went to have a peep.
T'matches I found and struck a light and looked on t'chimneyshelf,
T'pies weren't where we'd left 'em, so I thinks to myself,
I'm sure old Santa's got 'em! – as sure as dogs have fleas! –
Them lads at school was telling lies –
'cos my dad eats *his* with cheese!

And this is Clare's original poem:

To My Sister

Dis thoo remember Christmasses when we were lartle lasses?
We elped oor Mam ti mak mince-pies, an then we polished t'brasses
We shined up t'cannlestioks that breet, an put new cannles in
For Mam ti leet o Chrismas neet when Santa Claus cam in.
An then we gor a pie apiece an put oor awn mark on em,
An set em up on t'chimbleypiece for Santa Claus ti ger em.
We ung oor stockins up on t'post at boddom end o t'bed,
An then we thried ti get ti sleep becos me Faather said
"Ony bairn, at Santa indthers, gets er stocking full o cindthers!"
Wen we woke o Chrismas morn we ad nae cannle leet,
We gor oor stockins offen t'post, an guessed wi all oor might,
An then we shooted tiv oor Mam ti let us ev a leet.
She cummed wi t'cannle iv er and, er neetgoon lang an white,
She sat on t'bed an watched us undeein of all t'sthrings, -
She seemed as foorce as we were wi all oor lartle things.
There were pooaks o choclit pennies, an sugar-candy pigs,
An goodies, nuts, an apples, an rid-tipped sugar cigs,
An doon at very boddom, when we thowt we'd gor all t'things,
A lartle conny box apiece wi two real gowden rings!

An then we packed em up ageean an thried ti get ti sleep,
Bud Ah kept thinkin o t'mince-pies an went ti ev a peep.
T'matches Ah fun an sthruck a leet, an leeaked on t'chimbleyshelf
T'pies weern't where we'd left em, seea thinks Ah ti meself,
Ah's sure awd Santa's getten em! - as sure as t'dog es fleas! –
Them lads at scheeal was tellin lies, -
Cos me Dad eeats is wi cheese!

Another example of Clare's dialect verse is this poem about old Zebadiah, who gives words of comfort to patients visiting the doctor.

Awd Zeb Says

Awd Zeb, oor jobbin gardener,
leeans ower t' Docther's side wall.
Ti patients comin an gannin
E es comfortin wods for all.
"Deeant thoo be freetened a' yon, lad,
just tell in all thoo's telt me.
E'll ev tha bether i neea tahme, -
aye - oppin fit as a flea."
"Noo Missis, thoo's nobbut dowly?
Cheer up! E can cure all ills
wiv a dhrop o stuff iv a bottle,
or a.box a lartle pills."
"Ah sees em gannin in awf deead,
coughin an peppin, unsteady,
an Ah sees em comin oot, be-dad,
leeakin wicker already.
Boxes o pills an bottles o white
a friendly skelp on t' shoulder,
oor docther's bloke ti put em reet, -
bud, deng – E's leeakin awder!
Earin all them ailins an woes,
fratchin bairns, an belly-warks,
Ah reckons E could deea wiv a dhrop,
an a rist for a courla weeks.
Ah deeant werrit im mich me-sen,
Ah cures all but t'wife's bunions
wiv ard worrk, an early ti bed
on a bowl o yat bioled onions."

Home at Holme

Clare did not begin her life in Kilnwick. She was born Clare Hannah Ibbotson on October 25th 1904 at Holme River Head Farm in Holme-on-Spalding Moor. Her father was a farmer.

Clare never got around to writing a formal autobiography but, during her years in Kilnwick, she did write about her childhood days, before and during the First World War. In a manuscript of memories under the title "*I am Carla*" she explains how she couldn't at first pronounce her given name, Clare. "*I insisted that I was Carla*" she wrote, "*and Carla I have been ever since.*" Kilnwick residents, who knew her 50 or 60 years later, confirm that they only knew her as Carla Ellin.

We learn from the opening chapters of these memoirs about the death of her infant brother Tommy, when Clare was five years old. Later, a new baby brother, Edwin, is born. Overall, in this document, a vivid picture is painted of East Yorkshire rural life more than a hundred years ago. It is a small piece of social history through the eyes of a little girl living on a farm.

As I read Clare's tales I was learning, or re-learning, dialect words from my East Yorkshire past. I know now, for example, that a stoggy is a woodpigeon and a stee is a flight of stairs or a ladder; a foldyard is an enclosure for sheep or cattle and a seggy bowl is a bowl made of sycamore.

For me, Clare's anecdotes are entertaining as well as educational. She tells about softly-spoken Dick and Jinny who came with their laes (scythes) to help her father with the harvest. They would open out the fields so that the horses and reaper could get in without trampling and wasting any corn.

> *"One morning early I stole from the house and went to see Dick & Jinny. They were camped in a thicket of hazel and broom in the wood beyond the beck. Jinny was frying bacon in the flat black skillet suspended over the fire from a tripod of green saplings, thick fat salty slices cut from some local cottage pig, it would be. Dick was just getting over the fence with something tied up in his red ketcher. "Be thee coming to break thy fast, little miss?" he asked,*

"See what I got here, blue-stalks from the wood, and fine they'll taste with the bacon."

He cut off the soiled end of the stalks and dropped the trimmed mushrooms in the sizzling fat. The dainty blue fungi soon turned to a black-looking mess among the bacon. Dick removed his hat, broke up the cob of bread and, as he handed it to us, looked up among the tree tops and said softly, "Lord, we thank Thee." All my life no other Grace or thanks for food, no solemn Eucharist or convivial toast has meant as much as Dick's simple thanks.

I drank strong tea from a cracked jam jar at breakfast with Dick & Jinny that early morning. There was milk but no sugar, well there were cows in the field but no sugar canes and we were never allowed sugar in our tea at home. We rarely drank tea anyway, only milk or pump water. What my mother would have said about the bluestalks I dared not think.

When Clare needed solace, she would go and sit in her 'Thinking Tree' or she would crawl into Rover's kennel and talk to the dog. When no-one would believe her or listen to her, Rover was her sympathetic ear.

Clare began her education at home, studying there until her kid sister Dorothy, (Dot) reached school age and then they started school together, walking the three miles to Holme and back each day. Sisters don't always get on, however, and these two were no exception as Clare's narrative relates.

"But later I caught our Dot on the privy and I held the door shut so she was in the dark and I shouted at her, "Tell-pie-tit! Laid an egg and couldn't sit." And she nearly howled the place down. She told our mother all the tales from school about how clever she was and what teacher had said. Daft, she was. "And what has thoo to say for thee-sen?" my dad would ask, and I would sulk and say "Nowt". I could tell Rover, or climb up my tree and think but I mostly lost my tongue when they asked me about school. I was getting too big to get inside Rover's kennel to talk now so I had to sit on the stone outside. Poor Rover was blind in one eye by then. He'd had it bitten by a rat when the lads were ratting. They shouldn't have taken him, sheepdogs are not for ratting, they should have had a terrier.

Clare had both lots of grandparents in her life and knew them as Big Granddad and Little Granddad. Clare has one particularly vivid memory of Little Granddad from when she was about six.

"On this night I woke to some unusual sound. It must have been somebody going out at the front door for I heard the wind blow it open again and send it crashing back against the hat stand. I jumped out of bed. The curtains were blowing in the dim light like flapping great wings and when I opened the bedroom door and stepped onto the landing the draught from the front door blew my nightdress about my head. I groped my way halfway down the stairs, my eyes watching the oblong of greyish light that was the open front doorway and there, hanging in the rambler rose, was the merry face of little grandpa smiling at me, whiskers and all.
"Grandpa!" I shouted, got tangled in my long nightie and fell to the bottom of the stairs. It seems that mother heard me and was gathering me up when father burst in, slamming the front door fast behind him and driving the bolts home. I was hauled back to bed, the window was shut and I slept till morning and was none the worse for my fall.

Next morning at breakfast time Uncle Ted drove into the yard.
"Whatever's he want at this time of day?" mother exclaimed.
"He's come to tell us that little grandpa is dead", I said, "I saw him laughing at me last night when the wind blew the door open – his face was hanging up in the rose tree."

"Yes, the old man passed out at two o'clock this morning", said Ted.
"Aye, why that's about time I had to go out to t'privy - poor old lad" said father. "He was happy enough when he smiled at me," I said and they all looked uncomfortable and began to talk all at once. I put some more treacle on my porridge, twirling the spoon high up to watch the long dripping gold.

At school Clare was fortunate to have teachers – Mr & Mrs Tether – who saw that she had artistic talent and encouraged her to draw and even organised drawing materials for her. Later in life, when Clare was writing her reminiscences from her childhood she illustrated them with her own drawings, as you see here.

A picture of what Clare's life was like when she was around eight years old is painted in this poem she wrote many years later.

After School

Laughing, shouting, chasing! - freed at last from school, -
coats and mufflers flying, dinner bags aswing,-
snatching caps and ribbons, pulling girls' pigtails, -
sparkling eyes and laughing tears, rosy faces tingling!
Gloveless fingers stiff with cold,
feet benumbed in sodden leather,
we run with all the other children
down the street together,
stopping at the little shop
where Peter Bradley set on swinging shelves of glass
little china mugs and pottery pitchers filled with
foil-wrapped sweets, fairies, gnomes and red-capped elves,
jointed wooden dolls with painted fringes,
prancing pie-bald ponies, little wooden gigs,
chocolate coins and watches, and pink sugar pigs.
Through the steaming glass we see them
shining there like glowing jewels, and, behind them,
Peter peering through his spectacles, watching us,
our flattened noses pressing on the misted panes.
Green mints and stripey bullseyes for a penny!
Ruby-studded lockets, glittering golden chains
for a silver shilling!
But we haven't any magic to open Peter's door. -
No pennies in our pockets to squander on his store!
We look, then, sighing, leave our chattering friends,
leave the golden arc of luring light about the old
bow window, and turn our faces homeward through
the greyness of the winter afternoon.
Blood-red streaks of sunset in the sky behind,
Steel-bright glints of water in the lane before,
creeping fog dissolving shapes of fence and trees,
sheep behind the hedges coughing like old men.
Footsteps coming up behind! Stop! Listen! -
Only pee-wits crying over distant fields, -
no following feet, only muffled echoes of our own.
Hand in hand we run, leaving light behind,
forward to the darkness of the overhanging trees,

treading softly through the mud thick near the gate
where Blossom stood in honeysuckle time.
There, look! A great white owl on silent wings
glides slowly down across the lane into the leaning tree.
We pause to watch, then run again on tip-toe, and,
coming round the bending lane, we see
the twinkling star of home.
Laughing, shouting, running down the lessening way, -
Oh! gladsome ending of another school day!

Clare's thoughts often returned to her happy childhood days, just as A. E. Housman's did: "*That is the land of lost content, / I see it shining plain, / The happy highways where I went/ and cannot come again.*" The following three poems were all written whilst the author was living in Kilnwick.

February Moon

This is not the moon I knew -
the moon that lit my world with liquid light
when I was young -
feathering the fragile fans of trees,
blocking the farmyard shapes on snow,
and yet uneasing my mind with prescient
knowledge yet to grow.
Then, for a while, I held
the silent beauty of the sight
until the blasts of science
shattered my delight
in the magic of a February night.
Aye, now we know too much
and underestimate the stuff of dreams.

Candle Wick Trimmer

I don't know how I came by you
but I've treasured you for years
and now as I gently polish you
your pewter sheen stirs memories,
a chill of childish fears
when bedtime was a candle flame
shimmering through my tears.

Aunt-Polly laid her knitting by
to trim the candle wick
smoking in its tallow
with a trimmer just like this.
She held the new-bloomed candle high
to light me up the stairs
where shadows boggled up the wall,
then, when I'd said my prayers,
she took the dimpsy light away
and I shivered in the dark
fearing the shadows on the stairs
for they would surely stay
hiding in the corners
until the light of day.

Toast

The hot cinders spark soot
to scintillating fire flies
dancing their way up the chimney.
Souls going to heaven
Old Hannah said when I was young.
We had buttered toast for tea then
before she mended the fire.
And there on my wall, see,
hangs her old toasting fork
battered and polished
by hands long dead.
Brass beat to a twisted stem,
the grinning face of Old Sol
frilled with flame-petals for its head
and its three-pronged fork begging bread.
Hit! a toast to Old Hannah -
crisp, scorched golden and burnt sienna,
cinder-flavoured - a real fire toast –
fetch the bread!

In 1914, when the First World War broke out, the farm lost men and horses to the war effort. Clare remembers men going off on the train with a band playing and the men all singing *"It's a long, long way to tickle Mary"* and *"Goodbye Dolly Gray".* Young Bert, who had dubbed himself as Clare's Dutch uncle, also went off to the army and never returned. The army commandeered two of the farm's three horses. When they came to collect them, Whackem, who was a veteran of the Boar War, had them ready – and had himself ready too. Clare's father asked "Are you delivering them?" and Whackem replied that he wasn't just delivering them – he was going into the army with them. Off he went with Gypsy and Violet and that was the last the Ibbotsons saw of all three of them.

Whackem and Blossom

my Dutch uncle

The farm's shepherd, Chid, also became a casualty of war. He was trying to get his flock across the road when he was hit by an army car and killed along with two of the sheep.

Clare herself had a road accident too. She had been given a really smart Raleigh Rudge bicycle that used to belong to her 'fine aunt in Harrogate'. One day it suddenly jammed up and she was thrown over the handlebars, dislocating her jaw and smashing her face up very badly. Her little brother, Edwin, saw it happen and ran off to tell his mam: *"Mam! Mam! She's kill't! Our Carla is kill't!"* It took all summer for her to recover.

Their farm was never bombed during the war but they had to worry about being bombed because they had seen a Zeppelin come over once. Each night searchlights were scouring the sky. There was a strict blackout and a fear that Germans could land soldiers from the Zeppelins too - so everyone was on alert.

It was in 1917 that Clare was due to be confirmed. The Canon and his Curate rounded up Clare and her peers for a period of hectic cramming of the Catechism and religious knowledge. In Clare's words: *"This bored me to wicked thoughts."* Instead of taking notes on the Catechism, Clare started writing rhymes. One that she remembers was:

O God-unseen-yet-ever-near
Would you like a drink of beer?
My mother makes it in a bowl,
It's good, she says, for any soul.
So if you'd like a sup some day
Do call if you are out our way.

Clare dutifully goes through her Confirmation ceremony and describes the occasion in great and fascinating detail but says it didn't have the desired effect on her.

> *"I didn't feel good and helpful, as the Canon said we should. I was just empty and sick and not a bit sorry for my sins. Oh, there were such wonderful, beautiful things living and blossoming and happening about us, created by a very different God from the God-unseen-yet-ever-near spying on all we did, punishing us for all our mistakes, I couldn't love Him. My happiness was in being alone with all the wonders, or sharing them with father when he was relaxed and unworried. I liked that sort of God who made them all though perhaps he could have looked after some of them a bit better. "How can he?" said father, "there's ower much for Him to do by Himself. Me and thoo mun give him a hand when we can. I expect he has a good laugh when we don't frame very well. But he knows, thoo knows."*

In 1918 the Holme-on-Spalding Moor village school must have been a good one because when Clare won a scholarship to Beverley High School she was one of seven girls from her school to do so in that year. One of the other six was her kid sister, Dorothy.

Dorothy, Clare and Thornton 1918

This 1918 portrait of the three Ibbotson children together shows the two scholarship girls – Clare (14) and Dot (12) wearing the same dress. Their little brother, who was referred to as Edwin in Clare's memoirs of her earlier childhood days, is now using his other Christian name, Thornton. In 1983, when the Beverley High School celebrated its 75th Anniversary, Clare and Dorothy contributed essays reminiscing about their school days in those 1918-1922 post-war years. In those far off days, almost a Century ago, class distinction was alive and well. The Fee-paying girls and the Scholarship girls wore different colours of uniform and were accommodated in separate boarding houses. Here are some quotations from Clare's essay:

> *"We had to have dressing gowns, travelling rugs and hot-water bottles - luxuries we had never heard of in our Spartan farm life."*

> *"When differences in status or treatment annoyed us we consoled ourselves in the belief that we had the brains while they only had the brass - or their parents had. Their snobbery was unbelievable as they were encouraged to think that they were superior to us. If their elegant pale grey crocodile chanced upon the same walk as our blue crocodile, their Housemistress or Head Girl would contrive to avoid meeting or overtaking us. We never spoke when we met. We dined at mid-day in their dining hall in Norwood House but at a table across the lower end, and we stood deferentially as they filed out after the meal. Some friendships were formed in the classrooms but were frowned upon by the Housemistress."*

> *"We barely got broken into the school routine when the great influenza epidemic at the end of the First World War broke upon us. When it began to take toll of the day students we were instructed to write home telling our parents to meet us off the train in two day's time. By then most of us were ill. Blanket-wrapped we were bundled into cabs."*

> *"The spring and summer of 1919 were months of shortages of every kind. The U-boat menace had seen to that. Our rationed foods were put out on individual tin trays bearing our names."*

> *"Our schoolday crocodile in blue wound its way in the early days*

across North Bar Without and down Tickle-Belly Alley into Pighill Lane then around the corner into Norwood every weekday morning but on Sundays it was a dark blue croc that went through the Bar to Saint Mary's Church and sat at the back. Always early, we took stock of the fine gentlemen and fashionable ladies nodding and smiling to left and right as they proceeded up the central aisle. Choirboys hurrying up the side aisle to the vestry sometimes had a wink or a grin for us. Then, as the service was about to begin, in at the main door wound the pale grey crocodile of the Norwood House girls in their grey costumes and white hats. Slowly they progressed up the aisle to the front pews and we were sure that everyone was thinking what lovely girls they were, while we poor Scholarship kids at the back were wishing that our fathers had bags of money."

"In my third year I passed my School Certificate examination, but in the summer term of my final year I crawled back and forth to school with a continual pain in my side. Nobody seemed worried about it but me until one hot day I lay down under the walnut tree when fielding in a cricket match and couldn't get up. I was taken straightaway on a handcart pushed by the caretaker's son to the Cottage Hospital and became the sensation of the term. I had my appendix out and, in a private room, received teachers and girls like a film star in her boudoir."

"I missed the final Matriculation examination but was awarded a pass on the merits of my term's work. Back in school at the end of term I sang 'Forty Years On' with great gusto, packed my belongings, sold my books, and left the High School without a backward glance, let alone a tear."

One of the conditions for being granted a Scholarship at Beverley High School was that Clare and her parents had to agree that Clare would become a teacher and then teach for a while and this is what duly happened. Clare's résumé said:

"One year student teacher at Market Weighton Girl's School.
Darlington Teacher Training College for two years.
Teacher at Patrington School for four years.
Married Tom Ellin, an out of work engineer, and was dismissed by the

East Riding Education Authority on marriage. Daughter Ruth born 1931. Husband started own engineering and local agricultural repair shop. In 1956 bought a cottage with a large garden and reared poultry and grew fruit and vegetables. Took up writing for magazines, journals and newspapers.

Have regularly contributed poems to the Yorkshire Post, 1967-83. Member of the Yorkshire Dialect Society."

The cottage bought in 1956 was of course Oaks Cottage in Kilnwick.

This excellent professional portrait of all five members of the Ibbotson family in their garden was taken in 1920, when Clare (on the right) was sixteen.

The Ibbottson family 1920

This dialect poem appears to be addressed to a Mary Thackeray Wailer in Los Angeles.

Holme-on-Spalding Moor

An soa thoo's ta'en a fancy tiv a spot thoos niver knawn,
A lang naame fer a lartle place, the place weer Aa wer born!
Aa bet thoo weant believe me, but at Holme-on-Spalding-Moor
These eyes fost seed the leet o day i nineteen unnud an fower.
It wer t'farm called River Eead, three mile fra t'choch on t'ill.
At eight year awd Aa walked ti scheeal wi Mabel, Dot an Lil.
Oor beeats wer gowd wi buthercups at t'SprIng o t'year i May,
An white wi dust an cripplin tight o mony a Summer day.
We scuffled risty beech leaves, bunched conkers oot o t'shells,
But proper walked o Sundays wi Ma ti t'soond o t'bells.
We sludged through t'slush i Winther, brock t'ice, or made a slide,
An sometaames, of a Thosda, on t'potcart gor a ride.
Ther wer mugs and bowls, an pankins, an chamer-pots an jugs,
An Jimmy, tawd pot-hawker, lapped oor knees wi new pricked rugs.
E asked us riddles all t'way yam, an wen we asked fer more,
E'd say, noo, could we tell im why twas Holme-on-Spaldin Moor?
T'Moor, E said, wer a dowly plaace, a marsh o wailin bods
Wi t'land o Nod, an Wholsea, an lartle ooses made o sods.
An Holme, - it wer an island risin offend moor,
An Saxons, Danes, an painted men ad all been there afoor.
We larnt a bit at scheeal an all fra Mister Samson Feather, -
E crammed oor eeads fer scholarships, eight on us won together!
We wen tiv other scheeals an toons, we fun new friends an plaaces,
But Holme-on-Spalding Moor as still a few bemembered faaces.
An if iver thoo sud gan that way, thoo'll see aboon t'flat moor,
Choch on t'holme weer we wer wed, - me names scrat back o t'door!

Patrington

So we know that our East Yorkshire lass, the Beverley High School graduate, did not settle back in her home village of Holme-on-Spalding Moor. She went first to Market Weighton as a student teacher for a year and then on to Darlington Teacher Training College for two years. Clare was then given her first teaching post at Patrington School, where she taught for four years.

Clare first met Tom in January 1927. He was an engineer by profession, a bellringer on Sundays, and a musician on Saturday nights. He would come calling on his motorbike and they would be allowed to chat at the garden gate.

Tom Ellin 1927

These photos are from Ruth's family album: Clare in August 1927 in a new dress; Tom charming Clare's mother by playing the piano for her.

Tom & Clare marry at All Saints Church, Holme-on-Spalding-Moor on October 9th 1929.

On May 5th 1931 Clare and Tom's daughter Ruth was born. She was christened Janette Ruth in St. Patrick's Church, Patrington.

It was a difficult birth and that may have been why Clare and Tom had no further children.

We don't have too much detail about their life in Patrington but we know Clare lost her teaching job as soon as she was married. We know that Tom started his own engineering business and that Clare served as a Parish Counsellor. Clare also produced plays locally, such as J.B. Priestley's *"An Inspector Calls".* Tom was one of a team of eight or so bellringers at St.Patrick's Church where Clare and Ruth would regularly attend services.

Tom formed a dance band which was known as Ellin's Jazz Band and Clare wrote a humorous jingle as a tribute to the musicians in it. One of them was the piano-player Tom Guy, who was the organist at St.Patrick's for over fifty years. Another was the local greengrocer, Reg 'Nigger' Newlove, who played the violin. In the 1930s, of course, the 'n' word as it is now called, was in normal and general use by everyone and had no offensive connotations. Agatha Christie wrote her *"Ten Little Niggers"* story in 1939, and in the knitting wool and clothing shops 'nigger brown' was a popular colour to wear.

Ruth married Ron Brown in the beautiful St.Patrick's Church, Patrington in November 1951. Clare and Tom are on Ruth's left in the group photograph here. Ron was a Filey man and that is where the couple went to live after their Harrogate honeymoon.

November 1951

We know that Clare began to write verse to amuse herself when she was a child but it seems to have been only in the 1960s - and in *her* sixties, that she began to spend serious time writing and to have her work, prose *and* poetry, appearing in print. The only verse I can find about her husband Tom is this one that could have been written by many wives, including mine.

Morning Departure

Every morning you go from me
behind your newspaper,
away into some obscure realm
of high finance or bickering politics.
I sip my coffee alone
knowing you will return
in time to catch your bus
leaving a lost smile with us.

Today your paper lies unread
and away over your cup's rim
your eyes, lost in greyness,
view some secret place.
Your face relaxes, smiles –
take me with you, please?
But you are miles from here –
"More coffee, Dear?"

The above poem is on page 13 of her "*East Riding Heritage*" collection, in which the opening verse is about herself.

East Riding Lass

Nay lad, Ah's a Yorksher lass,
East Thridin' born an' bred.
Ah've na thruck wi' Ummerside
except for t'lad Ah wed.
'E cam oot of 'Owderness
twixt 'Ummerside an' sea –
an' that low bit o' country
thrue 'Ummerside it be.
But Dhriffil, Wetwang, Bevla,

Bugthrop, Killick, Thwing,
they never 'eard of 'Ummerside
till this new-fangled thing.
East Thriding folk we'll ever be,
ay, Yorrksher tykes, both thoo an' me.

Fate – and the East Riding Education authorities – sent Clare to Patrington in the late twenties and she spent the next three decades of her life there. Her husband was a bellringer at St.Patrick's Church, the town's famous landmark.

His brother-in-law was the organist and Clare and her daughter were regular worshippers there, so it was perhaps to be expected that she would compose a tribute to it.

Patrington Church

A thousand dawns have painted her
in rosy wash and golden light;
a thousand shining noons have etched
her traceries in black and white;
a thousand eyes have hallowed her
healing time's wounds and scars;
a thousand nights have silvered
her pinnacles pointed with stars.
Serene and stately through the years
of sun and, and storm and stress,
her slender spire still crowns the plain,
the lovely Queen of Holderness.

Like the above verse, a lot of the thirty-eight poems in the *East Riding Heritage* collection are about places, but Clare wrote many, many more poems on a wide variety of subjects, as we shall see later.

We have already seen that Clare had some skill as an artist with a pencil. This excellent sketch of Clare was drawn at Easter in 1953 by her equally talented daughter, Ruth.

Sadly, Clare has left us no book of memoires about these important Patrington years, during which Clare taught school, met and married Tom Ellin, and had a daughter. It was only after Ruth had married and left home that Tom and Clare started to look for a new home. What Clare was looking for - the thing that was way up on top of her 'must-have' list – was a large garden. When, after a prolonged search they finally found exactly what they were seeking, it just happened to be in a little village that used to be called Kilnwick-on-the-Wolds.

Kilnwick

So, in 1956, whilst British and French forces were moving into the Suez Canal Zone, Tom and Clare Ellin were moving into Kilnwick. They were both in their mid-fifties now – in the prime of their lives. As a matter of interest, Land Registry records show that the purchase price of Oaks Cottage in 1956 was £1,925.

The farm in Holme-on-Spalding-Moor, where Clare was born in 1904 and where she grew up, had been inherited by her brother Thornton. But during the decades Clare lived in Patrington her brother had moved to Cawkeld Farm next to the village of Kilnwick. Thornton's daughter, Jill had married Brent Flint and the Flint family now ran the farm. It was a pure coincidence that Clare & Tom's new home was in the same small village.

On May 1st 1963, in a local newspaper, under the headline *Dream Cottage Came True*, these snippets are parts of what Valerie Ann wrote:

> *"Mr and Mrs T. Ellin spent more than a year combing the Yorkshire Wolds for a small cottage with a large garden and, when they found the one they wanted, were not in the least deterred by the fact that it stood in a village with a population of 113, utterly remote from supermarkets and cinemas,and had a garden which would make the Amazon jungle look like a stretch of the M1. Maybe it was the four-leaved clover that Mrs Ellin found at her feet when they joined the army of those with orders to view, that accounted for their rapid decision to buy the little semi-detached cottage with the appealing corner windows and large, neglected garden."*
>
> *"The little Wolds village of Kilnwick, which views with suspicion strangers who do not know that it should be pronounced "Killick", consists of several new Council houses, a little stone church and 10 pairs of mellow-brick cottages, built in 1781, as homes for the workers on a now defunct estate. In one of these live Mr and Mrs Ellin."*

Ruth remembers her mother telling her that it was not only the sight of the four-leaved clover that she regarded as a good omen, but also the welcoming song of a wren in the Oaks Cottage garden that won her heart and made up her mind for her.

A year later, in May 1964, *Homes and Gardens* printed an article *A Garden for Retirement* written by Clare herself. This is part of what she said:

> *"When my husband and I set about converting the half acre of wilderness round the modernised cottage we bought when we reached our middle fifties, we had one aim in view – to make a permanent labour-saving garden for easy management as we grew older. It was to provide beauty, pleasure and food, with the minimum of work.*
>
> *The garden had been a farmyard and we took the line of least resistance, converting existing features with available material, and hiding and camouflaging snags and discrepancies, rather than working to a preconceived plan involving laborious clearances. Plum and apple trees, old but fruitful, dotted the north-east corner. We fenced in this area with weathered oak duckboards bought cheaply from a dismantled camp and planted pink and yellow climbing roses along it. We added new pear, apple and cherry trees to augment the old ones, built a henhouse and bought twenty pullets. Now we have eggs and fruit in plenty and a weed-free orchard.*

The photograph below comes from Clare's niece, Jill Flint, who also lived on Kilnwick's Main Street. Sadly, Jill passed away on April 25th 2016 as this book was being written. The three men standing in front of Oaks Cottage are Fred Suggett, Tom Ellin and Fred Coverdale. The trousered figure in the background is probably Clare herself.

Fred Coverdale lived in School Lane and was the man who would cut the grass in Killick's churchyard and also burn the garden rubbish there as he is doing in the photograph on page 28, snapped in all likelihood by Clare. Clare also wrote this poem about him.

Quiet hours

In the hot sweet morning
he passes - Old Father Time –
scythe over his shoulder,
on his wife's high rickety bike,
battered hat shading his
merry eyes, off to mow grass
in the graveyard.

In the cool of the evening
dun smoke curls up
the sunset sky behind
the grey tower.
There he leans on his fork
contemplating the red heart
of his dying fire.
"Aye, why, I like an hour
among the quiet ones," he'll say.

We have seen that Clare had a talent for drawing so it is no surprise that her daughter Ruth was also blessed with artistic gifts. Ruth's skill was to paint porcelain and to do it to an extremely high standard. So much so that she could copy a Crown Derby plate so that it was indistinguishable from the genuine article. She had her own kiln so that her work could be properly fired to fix the colours for eternity. When my wife and I went to see her, she proudly took Elsie around to show her numerous examples of her exquisite work.

In this picture, Elsie holds up one of Ruth's plates to the camera as Ruth looks on.

Of course, for Ruth, the porcelain painting was only a hobby and none of her work was ever offered for sale. Tragically, Ruth can no longer pursue this hobby because she is left-handed and the stroke she suffered some eleven years ago took away her skill.

Ruth's plate here is a painting of her parent's home, Oaks Cottage, on Main Street in Kilnwick.

In 1951, five years before the Ellins came to Kilnwick, Kilnwick Hall and its estate was offered for sale by auction. The reserve price on the Hall itself was £2,750 but no-one wanted the property at that price so, sadly, it had to be demolished. *The Lost Houses of East Yorkshire* (1988) said that this "exceptionally interesting mansion" was the greatest post-war loss amongst the East Riding's all too few country houses.

So Kilnwick Hall disappeared, but the magnificent cedar tree – on the right of the picture below – survived. This photograph was taken from a spot close to where *The Willows,* which was built about ten years later, now stands. So the tree forms part of the view northwards from my kitchen window. It is something of a landmark in Kilnwick so it is not surprising that Clare wrote a poem about it. *Cedar of Lebanon* was featured in the *Yorkshire Post* on 11 June 1977.

Cedar of Lebanon

How old are you, cedar?
Your dreams must be fables
woven since moonlight
lit towers and gables
now here in ruins
about your spread roots.
Peacocks and nightingales,
doublets and farthingales
kept you company through
years of your growing.
Pious pale faces
of monks and priests,
Stuart velvets and laces,
aristocrats, Roundheads,
pink, shy-eyed girls,

in ribbons and curls,
little Lord Fauntleroys,
bumpkins in corduroys
passed her about you.
Now, serene and alone,
you dream, dark one –
how old are you now,
cedar of Lebanon?

As already mentioned above, Clare's immediate neighbours in Main Street were the Robsons, Maurice and Jill and their two small daughters, Lucy and Sally. Maurice & Jill kept their garden and lawns in immaculate order. There was a gap in the hedge between the two gardens so little Sally, whose middle name is Amanda, could wander through into Clare's domain, which was deliberately somewhat less manicured than Maurice and Jill's pristine plot. This little verse tells the story.

The Gift

"May I pick some for my mummy?"
Amanda asked, stooping
to stroke the daisies
on my morning lawn.
"They are flat and wet.
Can I put some in a little pot
if you've got a little pot
to spare somewhere?"
We hid the chip in the lip
of the yellow egg cup
with daisy frills
and carefully she carried it
through our secret gap.
"I'm sure my mummy will like them.
You see, daddy can't grow daisies
on his lawn."
"Well, they do need a special magic,"
I said and she nodded,
understanding. "Yes"" she said,
"some things do."

Clare also wrote this poem below about the day a daisy died. We can only guess at the identity of the fastidious man.

Daisy

One small daisy, golden-eyed,
gazes sunward from
the fastidious man's lawn,
the only weed to be seen
on the shorn velvet green.
It offends the man.

He bends to twist its roots.
I feel its agony as sinews tear.
I seem to hear
its soundless whimpering
as he tosses it in
his new compost bin.

Never more will it see the sun
or feel the dew on
pink-tipped petals at dawn.
I think I dislike
the fastidious man
with the immaculate lawn
and the new compost bin.

In literature the majority of poems, as you might expect, are love poems. Of Clare's output, however, only a few touch on this emotion. Here are two of them. The first is a bit of people-watching; the second is a rare glimpse into the poet's own private world.

Young Love

Yonder a toy-like yellow tractor
purrs up pale chalkland furrows
in a silver confetti of gulls.
Behind us white sheep scatter
on a green slope as a girl,
dark hair flying runs down
to the lane clutching a pot
of geraniums - scarlet geraniums
on a high sheep wold?

No hand free to wave to him,
her voice lost in gull cries –
will he see her before he turns
with the sun in his eyes?
Yes! Yes, oh, yes!
He jumps from his cab,
leaps the clods between
and his arms hold the lot –
dark hair, laughing face
and geranium pot.
The gulls scream above
at this rapture of love
interrupting their dinner.

Old Love

She left the Morris on the brow of the hill
to wander the smooth surfaced lane.
Shorn verges, shorn hedges in neat precision
ran down hill then up again
with never a tree or a bush to impede
the patchwork pattern of fields.
Free, uncluttered, light-hearted was she,
and shorn white sheep kept her company.
With curious looks and twitching ears
they moved in sweet white clover.

She whistled low to them over the gate,
they gathered and looked her over.
She leaned on the gate to await the car,
she picked up a purple-sheened feather,
she stuck the feather in her hair
and her audience bowed together.
But when she laughed aloud at them,
uneasy, they looked askance
then tossed their heads and cavorted
in a playful downhill dance.
The Morris purred down with open door.
He smiled at the black crow feather.
She was tired and happy and seventy four
as they rode up the hill together.

Apart from her husband Tom, their daughter Ruth and family, Clare had two other loves in her life. She loved The East Riding and she loved Nature. If home is where the heart is, then her home was the East Yorkshire countryside. She appeared to have little interest in travelling to faraway places. However, we do know that she took a holiday in Scotland once because she wrote a poem about it which was printed in the *Yorkshire Post* in October 1979.

Whilst caring for her garden occupied many of her daylight hours, this industrious lady still found time to write. And still managed to explore the countryside around her, photographing it and writing prose and poetry about it. She also took pleasure in sharing her knowledge and expertise with others. She gave talks and slide-show presentations to Women's Institute's and Countrywomen's Association's meetings in village halls all around the Riding. Clare also became an active member of the Yorkshire Dialect Society.

Clare's ability to write authoritatively and entertainingly on country topics naturally came to the attention of local newspapers and radio stations, in particular *Radio Humberside* and the *Yorkshire Post*. At the beginning of 1967 Clare began to keep a scrapbook of her press cuttings. Over two hundred poems would be stuck into this book before she closed it late in 1979.

Her very first clipping was pasted, top left on page one, on January 2nd 1967. It was an article on home winemaking that she wrote for the *Country and Coast* column of the *Yorkshire Post*.

Country and Coast

KILNWICK, Driffield.

ON this January noon I salute the New Year. I hold summer in my hand, poured in a tiny glass. The pale winter sunlight sparkles through the blond wine, essence of a glorious May four or five years ago when suddenly, one morning, the countryside was flooded with the glitter and dazzle of molten gold. Dandelions flowed from the lawns, ran in streams along the roadsides, piled on the churchyard mounds, and invaded the meadows with a glare to burn the eyes. A common flower, a weed, but bold and handsome, derided by children, ignored by many, condemned by gardeners, but beloved of the home winemaker.

Miss that one scintillating day when the flood is at its height, and your wine remains a dream. Freshly-opened flowers are picked, stripped petals scalded, stirred, strained, coaxed and pampered with sugar, lemon, yeast—and patience—and in time they yield up this scented vintage of lovely May.

I have amber elderflower wine, too, muscat-flavoured with raisins, June's hedgerows laden with creamy foam above pink dog-roses, hot noons drowsy with sounds of bees and cooing doves — summer salvaged, bottled, labelled, for release in the cold dark days.

I give you a toast—An old-fashioned English summer!—C. F.

2-1-67

Clare's contact at the *Yorkshire Post* was a journalist named Andrew Weir, who wrote under the pseudonym, Northerner 11. Andrew and Clare rapidly developed a good – and a good-humoured – working relationship. Whilst Clare's prose pieces went under the *'Country and Coast'* banner, Andrew's column was under the heading *'This World of Ours'*. A week after Clare's piece, above appeared, Andrew included her poem *Imminent Spring* in his own feature:

> *"More than one client of this column has accepted my invitation to optimists to feel free to apprise me of any sign of imminent spring they see quickening all round them... The most spectacular report, however, comes from Clare Ellin of Kilnwick, Driffield, who confirms my impression that the birds are already putting on the bright colours of their courtship plumage:*

Imminent Spring

The world lay white and colourless
when I, at my window yawning,
beheld a flash of fiery hue:
a golden pheasant upward flew,
shaking snow from apple boughs
just as the day was dawning.
He puffed and preened his scarlet breast
with shining silver beak;
he shook his flaming golden cape,
then gave a loud demoniac shriek
rending the frozen air –
oh, how I wished that you were there
to hear the echoes ring!
And when the golden pheasants call
somewhere, soon, it's spring.
But sleep at dawn? –
there's no such thing
when golden pheasants start to "sing."

Of course, Clare probably knew more about country life than Andrew did and could, no doubt, have written his column for him if required. Andrew quickly realised how knowledgeable she was on flora and fauna, on herbs, herons and home-brewing, on voles or shrews, on daisies and dandelions, on spiders or swallows.

It was Andrew who aptly dubbed her ***The Wise Woman of Kilnwick.*** If there was something he didn't know, he knew who could tell him.

One of the themes of Northerner's column was the tongue-in-cheek, make-believe RGA, the Reluctant Gardeners' Association. This April 1967 article is a good example.

> *"Lest it be thought that the delights of hop manure might seduce me from my allegiance as President of the Reluctant Gardeners' Association, let me announce the award of this week's RGA gold medal to Clare Ellin for these lines, composed after hearing an expert instructing Women's Institute members on how to achieve the perfect lawn with the minimum of effort:*

Pluperfect Lawn

You too can have a perfect lawn,
Velvet – green and closely shorn.
Cut and roll it neat and flat,
Then spray it well with this and that.
The little ones, will they complain –
No daisies for a daisy chain?
Will Jenny Wren be at a loss
To build her nest, deprived of moss?
And, when I come to think it over,
Where will I find a four-leafed clover
Or even see, on summer morn,
My daisy-spangled dewy lawn?
No, thank you, sir, I'll use no spray,
But carry on the same old way
And keep my happy lawn.

My favourite Clare Ellin story is the one about the shrew. She wrote to Andrew Weir saying, "*This week, I found a wren's nest, out of which popped a pygmy shrew. In the nest were four eggs – and two new-born shrews.*

They were less than an inch long, with closed eyes, tiny ear orifices, and an almost transparent silky skin, through which their bone structure and pulsating organs showed. As I watched, the wren returned to the nest but when the shrew reappeared she flew away with cries of alarm."

Andrew featured this amazing tale in his May 31st 1967 column under the headlined question, "TOO SMALL TO BE CLEVER?" The article ended by explaining that it is a curious fact that the pygmy shrew doesn't seem to put herself to the trouble of burrowing but generally uses old mouse holes. The nest she makes is a round hollow ball, and the poor wren's ball-shaped nest must have seemed to this shrew to be the perfect prefab. Centrally-heated, at that!

Clare tells the story in verse, too, of course. In fact she wrote more than one version of it. The one that appeared in the *Yorkshire Post* article is not as good as this later, revised version.

The Shrewd Shrew

I'll tell you a tale that is perfectly true
of wee Jenny Wren and the Pigmy Shrew.
Now the little shrew knew that her time was due
and what was a poor little shrew to do
when the driving rain had flooded her hole
but climb up the twigs of the elm tree's bole
to the mossy nest with its round porthole
where Jenny Wren covered her four white eggs?
There were more to come but plenty of room,
so the pigmy shrew made herself at home.
With wee Jenny Wren she curled up to rest
on the four white eggs, and shared the nest.
Next day, when Jenny returned to her nest,
there were two small strangers, things with four legs,
"Tweet, tweet! Come, see!" excited she twittered.
"Where did you get them?" her husband stuttered,
"such fat little creatures! And soft as silk,
pray, what do we feed them on – eggs and milk?"
"Good morning! Good morning! You keep your eggs warm,
I'll cope with these, they will come to no harm.

Pop off, for I'm sure you have work to do.
we'll manage between us," said the pigmy shrew.
So Mr Wren from the tree top did sing
to tell the world of this wonderful thing.

Humour was a strong ingredient of the Ellin marriage. Clare would call Tom 'my familiar' rather than 'my husband'. And he might ask her, for example, "Would you like a cup of tea, hag?" If a caller enquired, "Where's Tom?" Clare would reply, "Oh, he's upstairs with Miss Gibson" meaning that he was working in his office. Miss Gibson, of course, did not exist.

There was always levity lurking too, whenever Clare and Andrew came together, so it is sometimes difficult to know how seriously to take what they say. This piece from the pen of Northerner 11 in March 1969 is a case in point.

> *"I didn't know the Wise Woman of Kilnwick bothered to read newspapers. After all, if you're gifted with second-sight as she claims to be, you know what the news is going to be before it's printed, don't you?*
> *However, her eye must have been caught by a recent headline on this column: "Spring tonic urgently needed," for she sent me a summons (by a pipistrelle bat, which acts as her carrier pigeon) to appear at her cottage.*
> *Her 'familiar', his lichen-encrusted hat pulled down over his furry face, was snoring in his rocker, in the inglenook. "Don't mind him" she said "He's still hibernating."*
> *"You had something to tell me? I said.*
> *"A spring tonic," she said, "I've never known it fail."*
> *She threw a handful of herbs on the fire, inhaled their aromatic fumes, fell into a trance and began rocking back and forth on her three-legged stool.*
> *"A drink for your green sickness," she intoned. "Take mugwort, pennyroyal, Roman wormwood of each a good handful. Boil them in two gallons of small ale wort, and when it's boiled strain it and work it with yeast. Then put in a pint of ye juice of scurvygrass and half a pound of horseradish sliced and half a pound of ye filings of rusty old iron. Let it stand ten days and drink a glass in a morning*

and at four o'clock in ye afternoon. Use exercise." She came out of her trance. "Got it?" she asked.

"Just one or two questions, if I may," I said. "I've heard of green sickness but I'm not sure what it is."
"A simple form of anaemia," she said, which gives a greenish tint to the complexion and causes your friends to eye you and say: 'You're looking a bit green about the gills, old son,' – as indeed you are at this moment."
"I felt perfectly all right." I said, "until you got to the bit about half a pound of filings of rusty old iron. That's a bit off-putting, isn't it?"
"There's nothing finer for the blood!" declared the Wise Woman. The half pound of filings of rusty old iron is the most important ingredient of the lot. The mugwort and the wormwood are just for flavouring."

"Before I pass this invaluable recipe on to my clients," I said, "may I ask if you have actually tried it yourself?"
"I've never needed to," she said, "But I physic my familiar with it every spring. As soon as he comes out of his winter sleep I tank him up on the stuff and set him to digging the garden over so that he can use exercise."
Even as she spoke her familiar whimpered and writhed in his rocker and was distinctly heard to emit a disgusted: "Eeeeyak!" The Wise Woman looked at him sharply, whereupon he instantly resumed his snoring.

Know what I think? I think he came out of his winter sleep some time ago but is pretending to be still in it to avoid being physicked with the rusty old iron drink. It wouldn't surprise me if he tried to keep up the pretence till well into July. And I cannot find it in my heart to blame him.

Clare's poems have also been included in a number of other publications. An anthology of poems entitled *Dialect Verse from the Ridings,* published by The Yorkshire Dialect Society in 1970 used three of Clare's poems: *A Man Bairn, Swaddin Peas* and *The Farmer's Lament.* And in 2005 the *Dalesman* published *Yorkshire Dialect Classics* compiled by Arnold Kellett. This assortment of Yorkshire poems, stories and sayings includes Clare's wonderful Christmas poem '*To my Sister*' (see above).

Feathered Friends

When I read the next poem for the first time, I felt it could have been written to me. Just like the Editor, I too have spent most of my life indoors, unappreciative of the wonderful outdoor world that Clare Ellin inhabited and understood so well.

To the Editor

I feel, dear Sir, it is not fair
you should be crouched in your
city office chair, or perched upon a stool,
while I, dear Sir, am loitering here beside
a stream of water clear
in scented light and dappled cool.
I saw a pair of coloured finches
gather blue forget-me-nots
to line a hidden nest,
I watched a partridge and his lady
kissing, breast to breast, -
but – could you ever understand? –
I held a swallow in my hand;
Now I whisper as he leaves –
Go, build beneath his city eaves –
Go, rest within his inky hand
and tell him summer's in the land!

Dawn Chorus

In the vanguard of day
comes a stirring of feathers,
a rustling of leaves,
an unfolding of wings.
A sleepy bird twitters,
distant cock crows,
soon the light brightens
and every bird sings, -
blackbird and thrush,

robin and wren,
linnets and finches,
pigeons and doves,
the chiming cuckoo,
the raucous crow, -
as swiftly westward
the ecstasy moves,
a whispering wave breaking
in grand crescendo,
encircling the earth
with the dawning day
over the cornfields,
the valleys, the woodlands,
and we turn in our beds
as it passes away.

Free-range Eggs

Cackle, cackle, little red hen,
You've been laying away again!
One brown egg in the nettle bed,
And one behind the potting shed,
A third brown egg up on the coal,
Number four in the elm tree bole,
The fifth beneath the apple tree,
The sixth on the lawn for all to see,
Number seven in the hay,
And eight where Moggy's kittens play,
The ninth one in the gardener's den –
Just one more egg to make up ten –
Ten brown eggs for the gentlemen!
But if you please, dear little red hen,
Do mend your ways and lay the rest
Here in this cosy straw-lined nest.
I'm tired of searching every day,
Besides, my dear, you should not stray
So far from home, - you'll get lost, sure,
Little red hen from Bill's, next door.

Greenfinches

A charm of finches chanced
along the frosted lane,
twittering, chiming,
a twinkling chain festooning
with scintillating drifts
of green and yellow
hedges with no leaves left.
Flutter and chatter,
hoar frost feathers scatter
as their tinkling chain
loops away leaving
the frosted lane
just a frosted lane again.

Stain the White Morning

The flaming cock struts in his shining world
of sparkling new snow,
Calls his hens to the fence,
Breakfast is coming.
The man with the grain,
mufflered, gloved, grumbling -
coughing the ice-splintered air,
kicks the wedged gate,
jars cushions of snow from the ivy sprays.
He is late.
Scatters blond corn frugally, kicks the
frozen trough noisily.
Curses. Catches the calling cock by his
proud flaunting feathers,
bronze-sheened, darkly green.
One outraged squawk, a scattering of hens,
the flick of a wrist,
a twist of the red-gold neck, and the round
golden eye in the crimson-combed head
is hooded and dead.
Scarlet flowers bloom and spread in the snow.
We need a dinner, you know,
the man said.

The Heron

A Chinese drawing
brushed on a backcloth of snow
the grey Fisher stands, motionless,
in water wimpled, slow,
white neck out-thrust,
black crest swept back,
yellow eye watching the stream
for the trout's arrow track –
a picture remote as a dream.

Do not move. Do not breathe.
No catkin shakes on the hazel branch;
no ripple wakes the sleeping vole
in his bank-side hole
till the lightning strike
of the piercing beak
skewers the fish
in the soft brown ooze.
One deft shake, a bang on the snow
and only pink-lustred scales to show
where the deed was done.

Thrush

Thrush on a gilded willow spray
how do you sing! –
flinging notes to this golden day
as if it were spring.
This is a false and stolen day
says the old sign-reader,
there's still more winter on the way –
this is a weather-breeder.
So sing your song on your golden bough
this fickle day
for every note of promise now
brings spring this way.

All Creatures Great and Small

Clare had a great empathy for even the smallest and most insignificant of creatures, and would observe them closely. This would apply at home as well as in the wild as these four verses testify.

After Dinner Observation

Light from tall windows
fell across smooth lawns
to meet the moonlight on the water.
At the sound of distant laughter
a reed blade shivered,
a fanned sheaf of reed blades quivered
and fell, neat as a redwood
at the cry of "Timber."
Ripples of silver spread,
a widening arrowhead
catching the moonlight,
as the dark velvet head
of the foraging vole
bore the sawn-off reeds to its hole
in the farther bank,
heedless of strolling well-dined revellers.
Hearing only the call of coots,
he ate his frugal supper of shoots
alone in his dark dank hole
in the bank.

Behind the Parlour Door

I flick my yellow duster,
I sweep the parlour floor,
But every day a spider spins
Her web behind the door.

Today she's been out walking
Across the parlour wall,
Pausing to get her bearings,
Doing a crab-wise crawl.

I fancied she was pleading
With sad and hungry eyes
For juicy fat bluebottles,
A feast of captive flies.

My heart was wrung with pity,
I promised flies galore,
I swore I'd leave her web intact
Behind the parlour door.

So if you think I'm feckless
With spiderwebs about –
It's just that I'm soft-hearted –
It's too cold to turn her out.

Chat with Cat

Grey cat with sable bars
and topaz eyes,
how you do stare.
Do I usurp your master's chair
where he smoked his evening pipe
and stroked your fur?
I would not harm you,
only charm away that baleful glare.
But now the red moon
lures you to the garden
to play tiger in the shadows,
or sit beside another cat
with topaz eyes upon the wall –
two pairs of topaz eyes
out-staring the moon -
with what intent?
Or will you caterwaul
when I am sleepward bent,
grey cat with sable bars
and topaz eyes?

The Caller

He came in the afternoon.
I found him standing on the mat
in his smooth grey coat,
no shoes, no hat,
in the gentle rain.
Come in, I said, out of the wet
or I'll bet Sally's cat
will get you.
He sat on the inside mat,
licked the wet off his coat
and tiny pink feet
then curled up and slept.
Next day he popped out
from a hole in the ceiling,
sat on the light bulb
watching me at the sink
and I think
You must go, Mister Mouse,
I cannot let you stay in my house.
Ill at ease, I set the trap
with best green cheese for bait
on the outside step.
Later his startled eyes
stared at me in surprise
and now
I have a sin to expiate.

Garden Poems

Whilst Clare loved her garden she loved wild flowers too. She also believed that a garden was for food as well as flowers.

Dandelions

All the wealth of Midas
held not gold like these,
the molten suns of dandelions.
Flooding the meadows,
flowing in dazzling rivers
along the highway's edges,
gilding the churchyard mounds,
glowing in clefts, on ledges,
gracing the torn rail tracks,
blazing unashamed, triumphant
among the garden's choicest blooms
where none can vie with them
for burning splendour;
beloved of the children,
the gardener's abomination –
You crafty ones! You hide
your seeding heads beneath my lawn,
ensuring future generations.
Dandelions – I salute you
with reluctant admiration.

Mint Sauce

Oh laggard Spring –
not one green sprig
of mint is there yet
in my bed of herbs
beside the warm wall
where Hoary Mint,
and Ginger Mint,
and fragrant Apple Mint

tangle with Lemon Balm
and Tansy,
come full Summer.
A small offering
of green Pea Mint
is all I need today
to garnish my lamb,
but only withered stalks
I see.
Bottled mint, dried mint,
are anathema to me. –
So come quickly green
with mint, oh, Spring!
and happy I will be.

Queen Ann's Lace

Queen Ann has trailed her petticoats
down every country lane,
leaving froths of filmy lace
wherever she has been,
trimmed with blue forget-me-nots
and campion posies pink,
with yellow lady's bedstraw,
to make the bumpkins wink.

Queen Ann, the generous trollop,
strewed her laces through the land
but now the Council reaper's out
with all its merry band.
The verges must be tidy,
the grass a smooth green bed,
the parsley lace lies ravished –
Alas! Queen Ann is dead!

We can be fairly sure that Clare, whose middle name is Hannah, is writing about herself and her own garden in this next verse.

Wild Garden

She left that corner untamed –
a place where the wild ones
could frolic in the sun, she said,
fearing neither scythe nor spray.
See the racemes of toadflax,
how elegant they rise
among the bedstraw,
see the grey-leaved mullein
spiring, dwarfing the scarlet silk of poppies
of fluttering poppies,
bluebells and pink campions.
Butterflies and golden bees
dance in the breeze
about the yellow broom.
Mayblossom and sweet briars
and honeysuckle scent the air,
and Hannah often lingers there
in her secret garden.

Winter Garden

Cold moonlight kisses the garden
white with sugared crest rime,
pencil shadows of ash tree,
pear, poplar and lime.

Plumes of birch rise motionless,
grey as smudge fires' smoke,
moonlight glisters pointed buds
with a delicate stroke.

The gables are pointed with silver,
the tiles of the barn embossed
with the crystalline shimmer
of midnight's magic frost.

When a Somerset-born friend read this next poem, she said, “Oh, I know what Lad’s Love is! In Somerset we called it Boy’s Love and my grandfather told me that, in his day, young bachelors who were looking for a likely lass to court, would wear a sprig of it in their lapel to advertise their availability.”

Lad’s Love

Lad’s Love and lavender
lead to Lucy’s door,
leaning over cobbles,
but Lucy loves no more.
The paper laddie swipes them,
scenting all the air;
the postman nips a silver leaf,
sniffs the essence rare;
the milkman leaves a bottle
beneath a yellow bowl,
then sticks a sprig of lad’s love
in his buttonhole.
The bobby leans on Lucy’s gate –
should he try her door?
Nay, Lucy’s safe with lad’s love –
Lucy’s ninety-four.

People Poems

Ploughmen

Ploughmen who've hobbled the clots all day,
feet lagged with clouts, blistered heels,
behind sweating hosses, for arrogant bosses –
none of you elegant town-folk feels
the ache of limbs homeward bound -
or if you do, you have fine cars waiting,
hot water, clean clothes and three-course dinners –
none of you knows what the short-cut meant
to the men who had dined on fat bacon,
whose children ran bare-foot to greet them.
You follow their tracks with packs on your backs,
seeing only the next man's behind,
hearing the squelch of his boots in the mud,
wondering where you will find
a dry place to rest and eat,
treading the blades of springing wheat –
and their women gleaned every precious head
to make bread for their children.
Why don't you walk along Mucky Dick Lane
where the going is good and easy and clean,
where pink cherry blossom sheds its delights
and sunlight filters new leaves?
There you can loiter in twos and threes,
lean on a gate and take your ease,
listen to birdsong and hum of bees.
Here's a thing I will tell you, Ramblers all,
my long life back that cherry tree lane
was a one man track through gorse and broom
a trod made by a shepherd
in sunshine and rain there and back
from his work again
but crab apples grew there then.
Please leave the lost ways to the ghosts that have been,
veer left at the brig with boot and stick
and return to your cars down old Mucky Dick.

Ramblers

"And where are you going, Sir," I asked
"with this colourful crowd behind you?"
"We're going a-rambling, Madam," he said,
"so if you've lived here all your life
perhaps my map may remind you
of old time footpaths and stiles
and kissing gates, when you were young
and gay, Ma'm?"
"Why so it does, an-all, me lad,
for I have come the primrose way –
the primrose way of poverty -
but I had no map to guide me.
I've plodded alone the nearest ways
from cottage to farm and milking shed,
I've tripped among the cuckoo flowers,
I've traipsed the dark before the dawn
in winter's cawdest hours.
These trods were made by them afore us,
by men and maids in the day's first chorus
of birdsong, and setting moons,
under snow-blinding skies, under leaden noons."

Retired Farm Worker

Twice a day he plods
across the meadows to the farm
to potter in the garden,
pruning, digging, planting, now
that his bullocking days are done.
Coat across his shoulder,
jacket and trews bound about
with band to keep out draughts,
he strides, head down,
through marshy places
to the plank across the beck.
There he pauses for his windings,
sees the velvet vole washing his whiskers,
hears him plop among the cresses.

He draws his pipe and misses nothing,
the buds of kingcups,
blue forget-me-nots,
the first pale cuckoo flower,
the zigzag flight of snipe,
the arrow paths of trout,
the mallard nesting in the rushes.
Three masters has he served there,
and still, coming up to four-score years,
habit takes him twice a day
across the marshy meadows
to help the missis in her garden.
And often of a Sunday
he wanders over with a pal
to view the blooming of his labours.

We know that Tom Ellin was a bellringer but this poem is not about Tom. But it could be about one of the Patrington team that Tom was in at St. Patrick's.

The Bellringer

One boot in the stirrup,
a sally in each hand
he chimes three bells each Sunday
and, by gaw, they do sound grand!
"Ah've rung sin Ah were a lad,
Ah knocked off then ti gan ti fight
Wi't waggins back o' t'trenches –
Oh, them shotten 'osses missis!
An t'blather, death an stenches!
Ah've been ringing ever sin,
callin em up for t'Sarvis.
They deant ton up like they used ti,
'cept for weddings an funrils
an Christmas."
One boot in the stirrup,
a sally in each hand
he chimes them bells at eighty-tree
an, by gaw, they still sound grand!

The Hostess

Tall and straight she stood
regal as an ancient queen
in her hand-spun gown
of moorland wool
a crown of soft white curls
above her aged face.
"No, I do not sit with people,
I do not hear a word they say,
I only sense unease at age disparity,
I'm ninety eight, you know -
when I reach a hundred
I think that I will go!
But you be seated and rest,
for I must greet the others."
Through the laughing, dancing young
she moved with quiet dignity,
her smile a wordless welcome,
her faded eyes a benediction.

The Telepundits

Here, in the privacy of our home
we see and hear three wise men
on telly expounding views,
arguing, interrupting,
interpreting world news.
Twitching nostrils, overflowing jowls,
looking wise as owls.
And I think how pathetic
they must look at bedtime –
big round bellies
cuivering like jellies,
hairy-legged, spindle-shanked,
unrestricted torsos itching,
scratching and twitching
after day's confinements;

fallen trousers, belts and socks
abandoned round their hocks -
and I tell them - enjoy your rest,
you've done your best -
it will just be as bad tomorrow.

Barn Dance

Ben banged the old piano,
Charlie beat the drum,
Maggie clashed the cymbals
as the folk began to come
to the barn dance
in Robinson's barn.
The old ones danced the polka,
the young ones smiled with scorn –
polkas, waltzes, lancers
were dead when they were born.
Ma Moody with her besom
danced a solo fling,
Jolly Miller raised the dust
in a madly whirling ring.
Old Tasker did a clog dance
with all his might and main
but the youngsters shrugged their shoulders
and ordered drinks again
at the barn dance
in Robinson's barn.

Village wedding

Sunlight through stained windows
on satin folds of her bridal gown,
on chaplet of buds on dark hair.
Veiled, she is Beatrice, Heloise,
-all the Romance of the Ages –
plighting her troth to her lover.
Unveiled, she is Katie, her solemn moment
held in tears' diffusion
of shimmering candle flames,
here in this little church.
Music, whispering,
shuffle of shoes,
fuss of photography,
nods and smiles.
Reception, greetings,
toasts and dancing, ribboned gifts.
Then flight at last under misted stars
into enchanted night.

When I read this reflective poem I wonder if *'The Woman'* is Clare herself. And if the *"the young mother nursing her child"* is her daughter Ruth with her baby son Robert. Ruth can shed no light on this for us so we are each left to make up our own mind.

The Woman

She lingered under the orchard trees,
hearing the bees in the sunlit hours
gathering their wealth from fragrant flowers,
weaving flight-ways through sapphire air,
the song-birds singing everywhere –
or so it seemed. And she dreamed in her world
of beauty and song
though she knew that tomorrow the wind could be strong,
that flowers and fledglings alike could die.
From her heart rose a cry –
have pity, do, on these fragile creatures
fashioned by you!
Were they mine I'd protect them -
but what can we know of His design?
Oh, how shall I know my God?

She saw the young mother nursing her child,
blue eyes wide in wonder gazing round, focussing no thing,
small hands twirling, pink fingers curling, grasping no thing.
The mother's eyes so full of joy for her baby boy.
A bright new spark from the Fire of Life,
from the Heart of all Joy kindled the blue
as he smiled, and she knew where God dwelt –
not trailing clouds of glory through mazes
of creeds and dogma where men
knelt but in the smile of this child for whose needs she felt.
And the woman said:
"I have found my God".

The Makings

"Good morning, madam,"
said the scruffy little man
standing at my door
with a frying pan.
"Do you think you could spare
a little bit of cheese
and some bacon rinds,
madam if you please?
I've got a brown egg
from your old biddy hen
and milk from the bottle
on the step, so then,
with a shake of pepper
and salt, I'm set
with the makings of
a good omelette.
But I have no match
to light a little fire,
so perhaps I could use
your stove to fry 'er?"
So I helped him out,
that scruffy little man –
five-year-old Tim
with his frying pan.

Times Past Poems

The Land of Nod, Holme-on-Spalding Moor

Once I spoke with an old man
who had spent his working days
drifting on laden barges
down quiet waterways.
He guided the blinkered horses
drawing long-linked freights,
plodding the narrow tow-paths,
resting at lone lock gates.
He drank at the landing tavern
here at the Land of Nod,
where merry bargees all agreed
there was neither Devil nor God.
Ever a good fat hen in the pot
and a kettle on the hob,
but getting back aboard, said he,
was always a dodgy job.
We came seeking the Land of Nod –
a signpost points the way.
We found the tavern, a farmhouse now,
the canal had passed away.
Hawthorn and elder have conquered,
thistledown floats on the air,
the waterway's grown with briers
and nettles are everywhere.
The roar of combine harvesters
beyond the lost tow trod
scares off the ghosts of bargees
who supped at The Land of Nod.

Three Miles to School

Our boots were gold wi' buttercups
at t'spring o' t'year in May,
and white wi' dust and crippling tight
on many a summer's day.
We scuffled rusty beech leaves,
bunched conkers out o' t'shells,
but proper walked on Sundays
wi' Ma to t'sound o' t'bells.
We sludged through t'slush in winter,
cracked t'ice or made a slide
and sometimes, of a Thursday,
on t'pot cart got a ride.
There were mugs and bowls and pankins,
and chamber-pots an' jugs,
and Jimmy, t'old pot-hawker,
lapped our knees wi' new-pricked rugs.
But now they ride in buses
and fight and rive about.
If they walked like we did
they might get tired out.

Shipyard Launch at Beverley

Six white ducks a-tipple-tail,
heads down in oily water,
tipple-tailing happily
seeking what they're after.

Shipyard workers homeward go
with greetings, jokes, and laughter,
the hull they'd fettled by their skil
launched without a falter,
had taken her baptismal dip
sideways to the water.

The speeches made, the champagne split,
the lords and ladies gone,
she sits there now, an empty shell
gilded by the evening sun,
six white ducks for company
heads down in rainbowed water,
tipple-tailing happily,
seeking what they're after.

A Place Name

Through t'woods, by beck and sea,
Ah've planned to go this place and that
For sure, afore Ah dee.
Ah've charmed mesen wi names at ran
A-trippin off me tongue, -
Just set em doon ti music
An they might as weel be sung!
But then Ah've fun oot, sadly,
That you can't gan iveryweer,
Soa, yan Ah've picked aboon all t'rest
An some day Ah'll goa there!
Mebbe it weant be what Ah think, -
Ah've ad sike dreams afoor, -
Ah'm aunted by t'quaint place Ah've missed
Called Holme-on-Spalding-Moor

A Miscellany

Calm before the storm

Heavy fulness of summer trees
humps motionless:
dun-bellied clouds
hang pregnant with rain.
Cornfields on every hill,
prescient of coming harvest,
having no rustle of sound,
no ripple of movement tonight.
About a shapeless hedge
a clamour of white convolvulus horns
seems ready to sound
the crack of doom.
Ducks crowd together,
a mottled cushion,
on an island in the pond,
Only one last little one
skitters on the green water
in a fuss of gnatting -
one tiny atom pursuing life,
fearless of things to come.

Blowing Barley

Come out, my Love, so early,
To see the blowing barley
On this summer day.
Barley awns, like golden beesoms,
sweep the foggy dew away.

Rolling waves on a flowing sea
The blowing barley seems to me,
Come, Love, before it is too late,
Come, sit beside me on this gate,
And I will tell you how I love you
As we watch yon barley blow.

Beneath My Apple Tree

See these broken fragments
turned again into the sunlight
by the bright-edged spade
beneath my apple tree,
this stemless bowl of
a white clay pipe
caressed once lovingly
by calloused hands
when some delving Dick
rested on his barrow
beneath my apple tree.
This shard of fluted china
wreathed with blue forget-me-nots, -
whose fingers curled about
this gilded shell-curved handle?
Whose lips sipped at this
egg-shelled rim?
And did she fling the cup at him
in outraged modesty when,
gripping his frail-stemmed pipe,
he dared to ask a kiss of her
beneath my apple tree?

Clare 1920

The Old Wish

Happy New Year. Happy New Year.
Plenty of money and nowt to fear,
A hoss and a gig and a good fat pig,
Please will you give us a New Year's Gift.
The New.
A Happy New Year -
Ring-a-ding-ding -
We've struggled through Christmas,
in spite of everything,
so buckle on your breastplates,
open wide the door,
for howling and whimpering
comes Nineteen Seventy-Four.
Smack his little buttocks,
tell him to get cracking -
there's work and wealth a-plenty,
it's only guts we're lacking.
With integrity and friendship
let's wipe out want and fear,
so here's to all and everyone -
A Happy New Year.

A Clare Ellin Calendar of Poems

January

Winter of Discontent

On Yorkshire when the sun was low
untrodden lay the crimson snow
and dark with menace was the flow
of rivers rising sullenly.
All night the frost in iron clasp
bound marsh and dale and wolds
and stilled the vapour breath of ewes
on hillside turnip folds.
Dawn spun shrieking whirlwinds,
blocking lane and road.
Men in their tiny toys gave in,
and up aloft the weather god
clapped clouds in maniac glee
and bellowed: "That'll larn 'em!" –
he's a tyke like thoo an' me.
But we can show him, if we frame
and he'll but free the sun,
that this winter of our discontent
will, like the cold, be gone
and we'll be ourselves again.

February

Raspberry Jam for Tea

Raspberry jam for tea,
and the blackbird I set free
from the net in June
eyeing a worm on
the wet February lawn.
That drowsy day
of brief forgotten summer!
Orange bill dripping
raspberry blood,
stained lips and fingers –
the scent of crushed fruit lingers
still in raspberry jam for me.
And here, blackbird, for you,
crumbs for your tea
on the wet February lawn.

March

The Last Snow

Curled feather flakes listlessly falling,
falling and whirling
like snow in a paper weight.
Under the blanket Spring is stirring;
daisies are calling one to the other,
each fecund seed swells,
acorn shells split at the thrust
of their embryo oaks;
spiralled green springs coiled
taut for release,
pallid looped blades,
shoots in sealed sheaths,
are throbbing and aching
in earth's moist womb, breaking
to birth at Spring's coming.

April

Spring

The word rings with bells on the air,
drips in rain pools tinkling and clear;
brings the singing of birds –
such billing and coo-ing –
and love's whispered words:
such springing and growing –
unfurling of ferns, unfolding of buds
in misty-aisled woods –
and the humming of bees in blossoming trees.
Spring's sun-gold spills on celandine frills,
from chalice of crocus and daffodils.
Sweet-breathing life after winter's death –
come gently with promise, oh Spring!

May

The Swallows are Back

They've haunted painted minarets,
they've skimmed far lotus pools,
they've peeped in latticed harems
(Which was against the rules!)
'Neath tasselled tents and canopies
they've twitted desert sheikhs,
And now they've claimed my woodshed
For weeks and weeks, and weeks.

There's a view across the garden
and it gets the morning sun.
I sit there in the barrow
to eat my morning bun,
but why the swallows claim it
and hound me out each year
when they return from foreign parts
is never very clear.
Perhaps they think as I do
that, travel where you may,
there's no place like old Yorkshire
in the merry month of May.

June

Summer Day

In the morning early
when the dew was pink
and pearly-grey
with the coming of the day
my footsteps brushed
the beaded dew
from lilac smocks
of cuckoo flowers,
and everywhere
yellow flags of iris grew,
and golden floods
of buttercups.
And then the sun,
its day-long journey
now begun,
kissed away the dew
with burning lips
and touched
with rosy finger-tips
the opening buds of May,
and gave to me
a summer day.

July

Heat Wave

The village dozes
in the noonday heat;
we doze on the village seat;
ducks doze, lined up in rows;
the beck dozes, scarcely flows.
The fat girl dozes
on the step before
the tall yellow door,
pink dress, pink thighs,
mouth open, closed eyes.
The thin boy dozes,
drooped on his purple bike
leaning on the rail,
wipes his sweaty face
with his grubby shirt tail.
All the place dozes.
From the dozing tower
the clock strikes the hour.
The spell broken, everyone
makes a bee-line
for the little shop.
Ice cream! Pop!

August

August

August has no identity
like flaming June
or dull November,
only a drowsy nonentity;
days full of bees,
the humming of a myriad wings,
butterflies in slatted sunlight,
and haloed things;
ice clinking in frosted glasses,
boats rocking on lazy tide,
blond feathered grasses,
and evening's last long light
starring with sapphires
the sequined gold
of the serene river
beneath a sky shimmering
with gnats' wings.

September

September's Here

Red apples bend the laden boughs,
freckled pears hang warm on walls,
ants and wasps make frenzied forays
before the dew of evening falls.
About the faded lavender
painted ladies, red admirals,
dance their last flirtatious ballet
with furry bees and tortoise-shells.
Red-hot pokers, golden-rod,
chrysanthemums and purple asters –
where has all the summer gone? -
Autumns coming, faster, faster.

October

There's nothing sober about October.
He's a randy old goat
in a tattered coat,
with fog in his throat;
wart and wrinkle,
sloe-eyed twinkle,
beery froth on his breath,
jewelled drops sparkling
his cobwebbed beard.
Crab-apples blush where
his eyes have leered;
chestnuts split their shells laughing
to see him cavorting,
coughing and snorting,
chasing beckoning dryads
and splashing nymphs
through forests and streams
where, eluding his schemes
for amorous dally,
thy swirl and twirl away
down each valley.
Ay, October's a gay old fellow
in a raggedy coast of rust and yellow.

November

Remembrance

They climbed the lane together
on their daily walk,
two veterans of World War One,
trimmed ashplants helping them along.
Suddenly, there in mid November,
at the stony roadside, scarlet poppies
spilled a pool of blood.
Bowed and cap-less there they stood
remembering,
Remembering rifles, bayonets, stenches
in the muddy Flanders trenches,
joking of Jerries, sergeants, shells
and all the hells of vermin,
filth and misery.
Then homeward they marched
shouldering their ashplant arms,
singing a song --
it was all so long ago
when they were very young.

December

Baby Claire - Christmas 1977

She kicked on the rug in the fire light,
the dark haired baby of our delight,
beneath the stars of the Christmas tree,
Christmas then meant more to me,
than all that money could buy,
more than all the carols and bells,
presents and baubles and tawdry tinsels,
except perhaps the woolly sheep
and the donkey that guards
her awake or asleep.
But the moment passed, the magic died,
the lights went on and Baby Claire cried.
Then in the comfort of mother's arms,
she took to the bottle sweet and warm
and drank good cheer to us all.

Talk of Death

In December 1954 Clare went into a Hull hospital to have a hysterectomy. She should have been home again before Christmas but things did not quite go to plan. She developed peritonitis. On Christmas day the hospital called. Ruth answered the phone but they insisted on talking only to Tom. When Ruth brought her father in from the garden he was told to come immediately to the hospital. Clare's condition was giving rise to real fears that she was about to die – and perhaps she did. This poem tells of the journey she took whilst she lay unconscious on that sick bed.

The Journey

I left this world on a journey once,
whiles ago and miles away.
A white raft bore me
on a soundless sea.
On grey swells of ocean
I lifted and slipped
down curved hollows,
slid over thin shallows
of shades through glades
of nothingness where light
was a frail mist of motion.
A star glimmered far
but I never got there.
They'll never know where I went
but when I came back you were there
on the hospital chair,
anxious with fear, by my bed.
When I go again I shall know
the way to the star
but they will tell you
I am dead.

Some time afterwards Clare spoke to Ruth about this out-of-body journey in which Clare was able to look down on herself from above as she lay lifeless in her bed. Clare spent a long period in a Withernsea convalescent home before she was fully recovered. Happily, she lived for another thirty, extremely happy and productive, years. Twenty-two years later, in Kilnwick, Clare wrote a more humorous verse on death. It was printed in the *Yorkshire Post* in September 1976.

Spent

The time has come, the old one said,
to speak of many things,
of wills and banks and properties,
of trinkets and gold rings.
But where's the use, my dear ones?
You see, I haven't any.
The gasman, coalman, taxman
have taken every penny.
Just send me up in holy smoke
upon my funeral pyre,
and laugh and dance
at my last chance
to set the world on fire.

In 1984, when Clare went into Driffield Hospital on what she knew was to be her final journey, she left this 'Final Request' on the mantelpiece in Oaks Cottage. And, after she died, on May 13th 1984 that was where Ruth found it.

Final Request

When I am dead, my dear ones,
cremate my deadness, please,
in warmth, with joyful music
for your comfort and your ease.
Remember the lovely times we had
and let no solemn person
confuse you in meshes
of outworn creeds and miseries.
I shall have BEEN
I will have GONE
I'll leave no irksome duties –
grave to tend or lettered stone
to litter the earth –
only a few written words
for what they may be worth
to those who care to read them.
Maybe there will be
a little tallow for a candle
and a handful of ash for my roses
but I shall be free –
or my tiny flame snuffed forever.

Acknowledgements

This tribute to Clare Ellin could not have been compiled without the unstinting help, support and encouragement of her daughter Ruth Brown in Derbyshire. Ruth has supplied much of the material and answered my many questions. I am particularly indebted to my neighbour, Richard Benwell of Kilnwick Gardens, who has lived in the same house for the whole 70 years of his life. No one knows the village better. Richard was the only Kilnwick resident to keep in touch with Ruth after her mother died. I also have to thank Kilnwick resident Rob Lee who now occupies Oaks Cottage and Jill and Maurice Robson, who were Clare and Tom Ellin's neighbours on Main Street. I am also grateful to Justine Greenaway for her secretarial assistance.